MINIBEASTS UP CLOSE

Head Lice
Up Close

Robin Birch

www.raintreepublishers.co.uk
Visit our website to find out more information about **Raintree** books.

To order:
☎ Phone 44 (0) 1865 888112
🖹 Send a fax to 44 (0) 1865 314091
💻 Visit the Raintree Bookshop at **www.raintreepublishers.co.uk** to browse our catalogue and order online.

Published in 2004 by Heinemann Library
a division of Harcourt Education Australia,
18–22 Salmon Street, Port Melbourne Victoria 3207 Australia
(a division of Reed International Books Australia Pty Ltd,
ABN 70 001 002 357).
Visit the Heinemann Library website @
www.heinemannlibrary.com.au

First published in Great Britain by Raintree,
Halley Court, Jordan Hill, Oxford OX2 8EJ,
part of Harcourt Education.
Raintree is a registered trademark of Harcourt Education Ltd.

 A Reed Elsevier company

Editorial: Carmel Heron, Anne McKenna
Design: Stella Vassiliou, Marta White
Photo research: Jes Senbergs, Wendy Duncan
Illustrations: Rob Mancini
Production: Tracey Jarrett

Typeset in Officina Sans 19/23 pt
Pre-press by Digital Imaging Group (DIG)
Printed in China by WKT Company Ltd.

The paper used to print this book comes from sustainable resources.

National Library of Australia Cataloguing-in-Publication data:

Birch, Robin.
    Head lice up close.

    Includes index.
    For primary students.
    ISBN 1 74070 191 7.

    1. Pediculosis - Juvenile literature. 2. Lice - Control - Juvenile literature. 3. Hair - Care and hygiene - Juvenile literature. I. Title. (Series : Birch, Robin. Minibeasts up close).

616.57

Acknowledgements
The publisher would like to thank the following for permission to reproduce photographs: AAP: p. **29**; CORBIS/Jim Zuckerman: p. **15**; Great Southern Stock/Denis Crawford: p. **24**; National Geographic: p. **7**; photolibrary.com: p. **25**, /OSF: pp. **10, 15**, /OSF/London Scientific Films: p. **26**, /OSF/Scott Camazine: p. **27**; Science Photo Library: pp. **11, 14**, /Mark Clarke: p. **28**, /CNRI: p. **18**, /Dr Chris Hale: pp. **6, 22**, /J.C Revy: pp. **16, 17**, /St Bartholomew's Hospital: p. **4**, /David Scharfe: p. **23**, /Andrew Syred: p. **9**, /VVG: pp. **5, 12, 19**.

Cover photograph of a human head louse on a hair reproduced with permission of photolibrary.com/Eye of Science.

Every attempt has been made to trace and acknowledge copyright. Where an attempt has been unsuccessful, the publisher would be pleased to hear from the copyright owner so any omission or error can be rectified.

Contents

Amazing head lice! 4

Where do head lice live? 6

Head lice body parts 8

Head lice mouthparts 10

Feeding needles 12

Antennae and eyes 14

The thorax and abdomen 16

Legs for moving 18

Inside a head louse 20

Head lice eggs 22

Laying and hatching eggs 24

Young head lice 26

Head lice and us 28

Find out for yourself 30

Glossary 31

Index 32

Any words appearing in bold, **like this**, are explained in the Glossary.

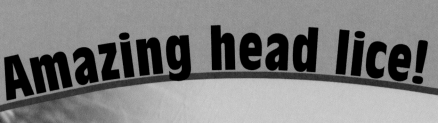

Amazing head lice!

Does your head feel itchy? If the itching will not go away, you may have head lice in your hair.

Head lice are so small it is hard to see them clearly, but they are amazing if you see them close up. They have strong legs with a claw on the end. In their mouth they have tiny needles for sticking into skin.

Head lice attach themselves to people's hair. They are sometimes called 'nits', but the nits are the eggs of the head lice.

What are head lice?

Head lice are insects. Insects are animals that have six legs. Insects also have a hard skin called an **exoskeleton** on the outside of the body, instead of bones on the inside.

There are many different kinds, or **species**, of lice. They live on many different animals. Usually, each species of lice lives only on one kind of animal. There is only one species of head louse.

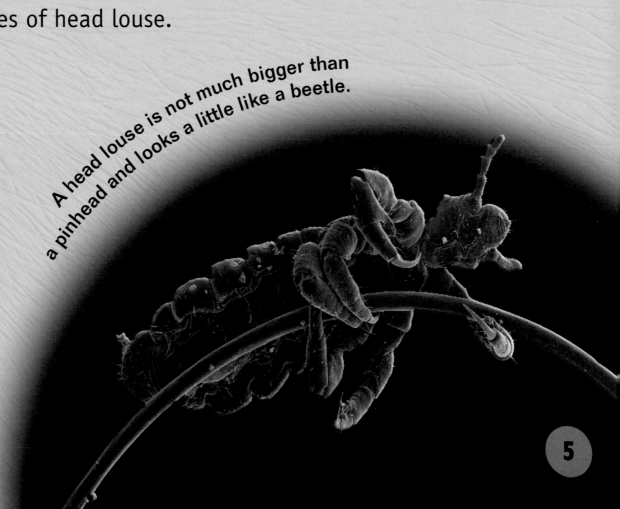

A head louse is not much bigger than a pinhead and looks a little like a beetle.

Where do head lice live?

Head lice are found all around the world, wherever there are people. They are more often found living on children than on adults.

Head lice mainly live on the head hairs and neck hairs of people. They live on clean hair and dirty hair.

Head lice usually live and lay their eggs close to the skin, where it is warmest.

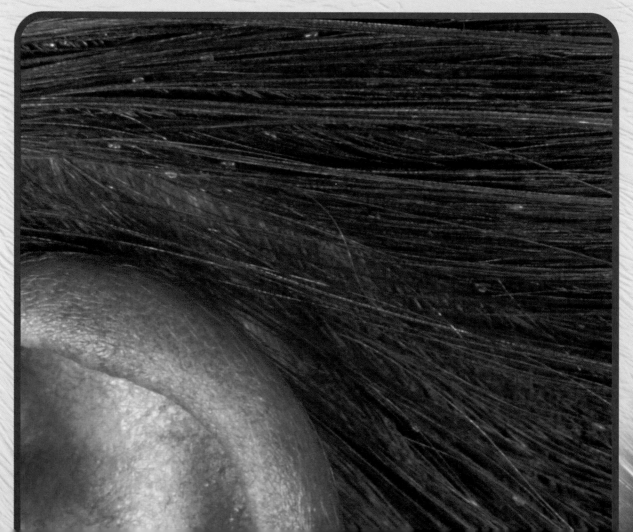

Can head lice live anywhere else?

Head lice can live on clothing, sheets, pillows, hats, combs and hairbrushes. But they will die if they are away from the human head for more than 24 to 36 hours. This is because they need to drink blood every day to live.

Head lice are not usually found on other parts of the human body.

Head lice can only live for a short time away from hair.

Head lice body parts

A head louse has three body parts. They are the head, the **thorax** and the **abdomen** (<u>ab</u>-da-men).

The head has mouthparts, two eyes and two feelers called **antennae** (an-<u>ten</u>-ay). There are six legs joined to the thorax. The abdomen is wide and flat.

A head louse's colour is between red-brown and light grey. It does not have wings.

Human body lice

A human body louse hides in people's clothes and also lays its eggs in clothing. It bites people's skin. It looks almost the same as a head louse, but its antennae and legs are a little longer.

Exoskeleton

The **exoskeleton** covers all of a head louse's body. It gives the head louse its shape and protects it from being hurt. It stops the head louse from drying out by trapping water inside its body. A head louse has hairs and **spines** on its exoskeleton.

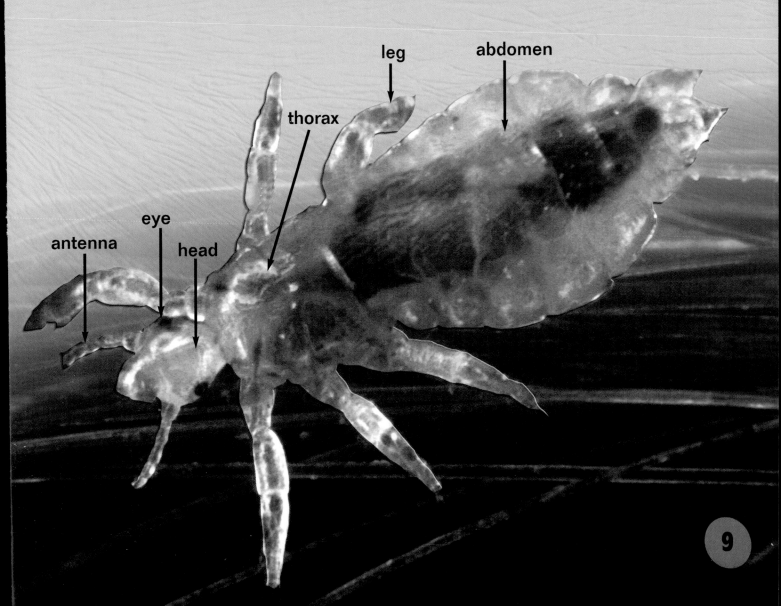

leg

abdomen

thorax

eye

antenna

head

Head lice mouthparts

Head lice feed on human blood. They drink blood one or more times a day. Without food, they can only live for about 24 hours.

When the proboscis is short, it looks like a bump on the front of the louse's head.

A head louse has a tube on its mouth for sucking in blood. This tube is called a **proboscis** (pro-<u>bos</u>-kis). The proboscis is soft, and it has sharp teeth inside the end. When the head louse is not feeding, the proboscis is short.

Hooking onto skin

When a head louse feeds, it puts its head down towards the skin. It stretches out its proboscis. The end of the proboscis turns inside out, so that its teeth are on the outside. It hooks its teeth into the skin, so its head is held firmly onto the skin.

Dog lice

Dog lice live on dogs. They have biting and chewing mouthparts instead of sucking mouthparts. They eat dogs' skin by chewing it.

Feeding needles

A head louse has three long, thin feeding needles. It keeps them inside a long bag in its head. The needles are about as long as its head.

When a head louse has hooked its **proboscis** onto some skin, it uses strong muscles in its head to push the needles out through the middle. The needles cut the skin and poke into it.

The feeding needles are kept inside a long bag inside the louse's head.

Sucking up blood

Two of the needles fit together to make a tube.
The head louse sucks up blood through this tube.
The blood goes into its mouth.

Itchy saliva

While the head louse is drinking, **saliva** flows down
from its mouth to the person's skin. It flows along
between the needles. The saliva keeps the blood inside
the skin runny, so the head louse can drink it. The
saliva can also make the person's skin itchy.

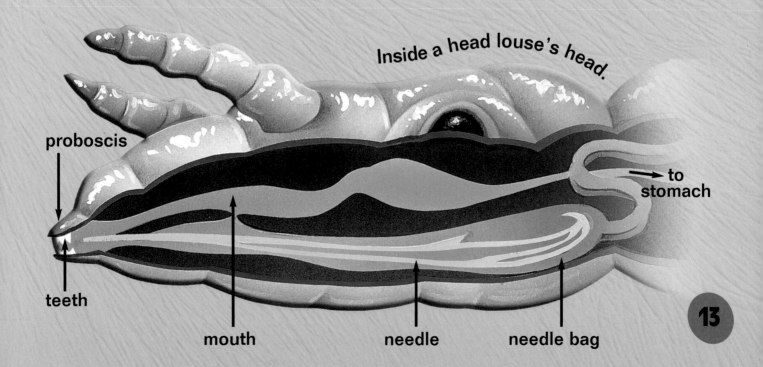

Inside a head louse's head.

proboscis

to stomach

teeth

mouth

needle

needle bag

Antennae and eyes

A head louse uses **antennae**, hairs and eyes to **sense** things.

Antennae

A head louse has two feelers called antennae on its head. They are in front of the eyes, and just below them. The antennae are short and have hairs on them. A head louse touches things and smells with its antennae.

A head louse needs to live and lay its eggs where it is warm. It uses its antennae to find out where it is warm.

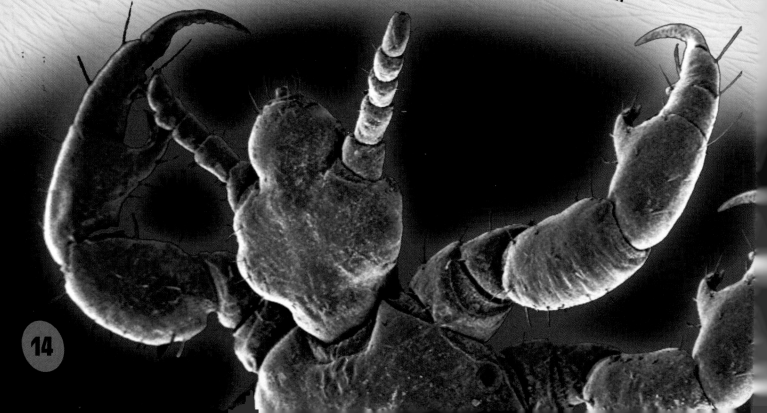

Hairs

A head louse has many hairs on its body. With these hairs, it can feel movements in the air and in the hair it is walking on.

Eyes

A head louse has two small eyes. It probably does not see very well with these eyes. It will run quickly away from light, so it must be able to see light.

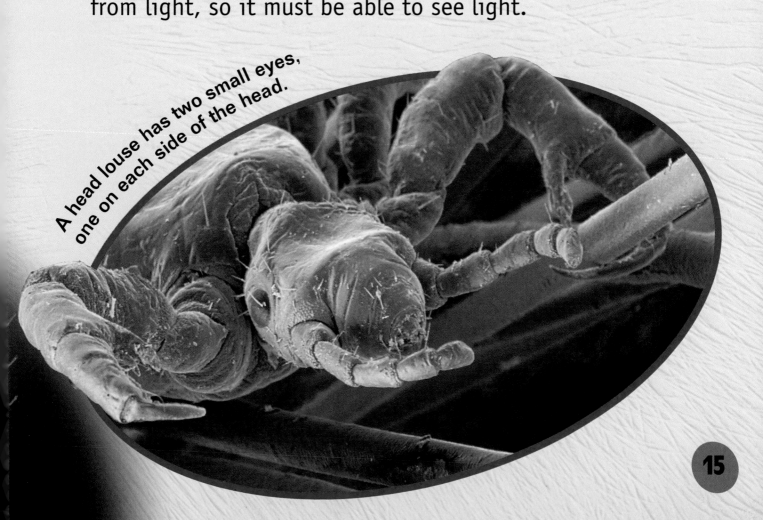

A head louse has two small eyes, one on each side of the head.

The thorax and abdomen

The **thorax** is the middle part of the head louse's body, and the **abdomen** is the end part.

The thorax

A head louse's thorax has six legs joined to it. There are two air holes, called **spiracles** (<u>spi</u>-rak-els), on the thorax.

The abdomen

The abdomen is wide and flat with seven sections. There are six spiracles down each side of the abdomen.

A female head louse. Female head lice are usually larger than males.

Male and female abdomen

The male head louse has a dark band across the middle part of each section of the abdomen. The end of the male's abdomen comes to a point.

The female has a wider abdomen than the male. The end of the female's abdomen has two small rounded parts sticking out, one on each side.

Colour

A head louse's body is often dark in colour when it is living on dark hair. It is often a light colour when living in light hair.

A male head louse.

17

Legs for moving

A head louse grips onto hair, and walks or runs along it. A head louse can also hold onto other things, such as hats, combs and pillows.

A head louse has six legs, which are joined to its **thorax.** The legs are short and strong. Each leg has four parts and a short foot on the end.

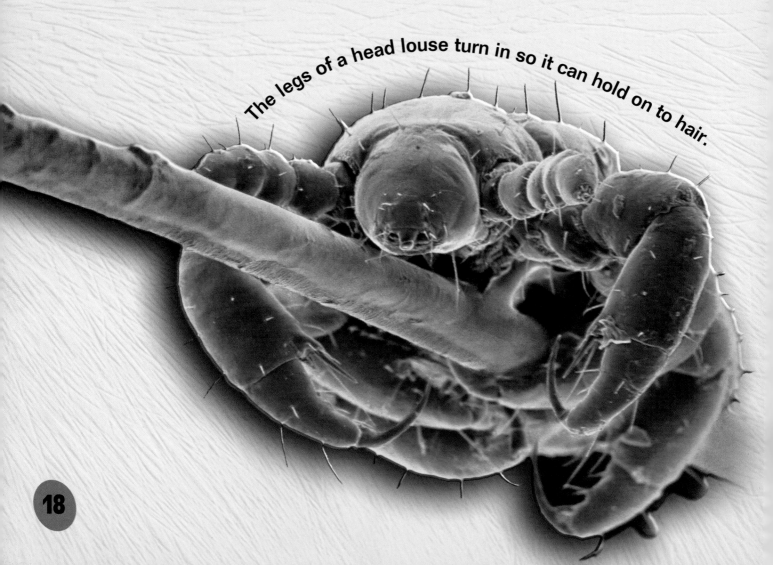

The legs of a head louse turn in so it can hold on to hair.

18

Holding on

A head louse has a large claw on each foot, which can be folded in. The claw is rough on the inside to help it grip hair.

There is a thumb on the end of the legs, just before the foot. The thumb has **spines** and hairs on it. The head louse holds a person's hair tightly between its claw and its thumb.

claw

thumb

Fast movers

Head lice can run very fast along hair. They move slowly if they are off the head. A head louse can easily walk from one person's head to another if their hair is touching. It cannot jump across from head to head.

Inside a head louse

A head louse has 12 air holes, or **spiracles**, on its **abdomen** and two on its **thorax**. It takes in air through these holes. Tiny tubes then carry the air around the body.

The heart

A head louse's heart is near the end of the abdomen. The heart pumps clear blood around the body.

What happens to food?

A head louse's throat makes a strong pump for sucking up blood. This blood goes to the stomach, for the head louse to **digest**. The stomach is long, and is in the thorax and abdomen. When it is full of blood, it fills up a lot of the abdomen.

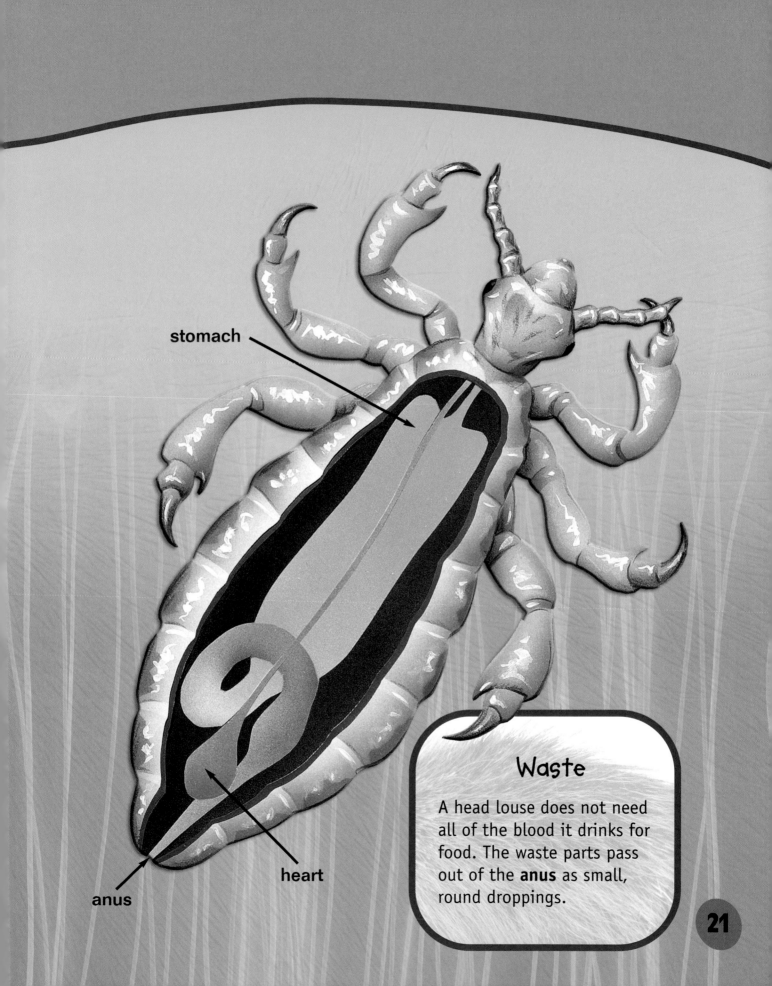

stomach

heart

anus

Waste

A head louse does not need all of the blood it drinks for food. The waste parts pass out of the **anus** as small, round droppings.

21

Head lice eggs

A female head louse lays eggs, called nits, in the hair.

Fertilization

Only the eggs that have been **fertilized** will hatch. Eggs are fertilized if the female **mates** with a male before she lays them. If they are not fertilized, they do not hatch.

A female head louse can lay up to six eggs every day. During her life, which may be 30 days long, she can lay about 100 eggs in total.

What is an egg like?

A head louse egg is a similar shape to a chicken's egg. It is wider at one end. It is yellow-white in colour, and a little smaller than a poppy seed (0.8 millimetres in length).

The wide end of the egg has a round cap. The cap has tiny holes in it that let air inside for the young louse. The cap comes off in one piece when the egg hatches.

A head louse with an egg.

Laying and hatching eggs

The female head louse lays her eggs onto hairs close to a person's **scalp**, where it is warm enough for the lice inside to grow. She most often lays them on the hair behind the ears and on the top of the head.

A head louse with a newly laid egg.

Eggs stuck in the hair

Empty and unhatched eggs stay on the hair, because they are glued on firmly. As the hair grows, the unhatched and empty eggs grow further from the skin.

How are eggs laid?

A female head louse lays her eggs in rows along hairs, with the wider ends of the eggs pointing away from the skin.

When an egg is laid it has glue on it, which comes from inside the female's **abdomen**. The glue holds the egg to the hair.

How eggs hatch

The eggs hatch after about eight days. The young lice use two tiny teeth on the front of their head to push the cap off their eggs, and they climb out.

This head louse is hatching from its egg.

Young head lice

Young head lice are called **nymphs** (nimfs). When they hatch out of their eggs, nymphs are tiny and have no colour.

Nymphs must feed within 45 minutes of hatching, or they will die. When they feed, they turn a red-brown colour from the blood they are drinking.

This nymph is hatching from its egg.

Growing up

The skin, or **exoskeleton**, of the growing nymph is firm. It protects the nymph, but stops it from growing very much. When the nymph gets too big for its skin, the skin splits open, and the nymph crawls out of it. This is called moulting.

A growing nymph moults three times. Each time, its body becomes larger. It takes about nine to twelve days for it to grow into an adult.

An adult head louse lives for about 30 days.

Nymphs look similar to adults, except they are smaller – about as big as a full stop.

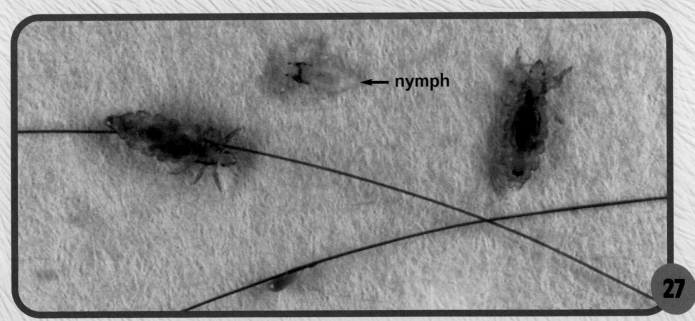

← nymph

27

Head lice and us

People catch head lice from someone else who has them. Children get head lice more often than adults, because children are more likely to let their hair touch other people's, or share hair brushes and hats.

How many lice?

Usually a person with head lice only has up to twelve adult lice living on their head. They can have hundreds of eggs in their hair. The eggs are much easier to see than the head lice.

Head lice like to live in clean hair more than dirty hair. If someone has head lice, it does not mean they are dirty.

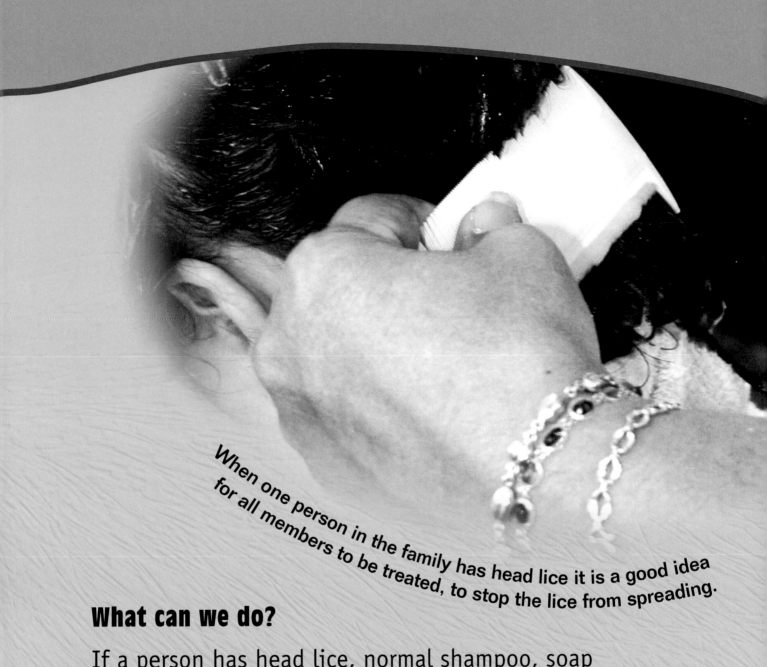

When one person in the family has head lice it is a good idea for all members to be treated, to stop the lice from spreading.

What can we do?

If a person has head lice, normal shampoo, soap and hot water will not kill the lice or the eggs. Brushing the hair does not get rid of them either.

To kill head lice we need to use special shampoos, creams and combs.

Find out for yourself

A child in your family may have head lice. If so, ask an adult if they could put one or two of the child's hairs, with nits on it, in a jar with a lid. Then you can look at the nits close-up, without them touching your hair.

Book to read

Bug Books: Head Louse, K Hartle, C Macro and P Taylor (Heinemann Library, 2000)

Using the Internet

Explore the Internet to find out more about head lice. Websites can change, so if the links below no longer work, do not worry. Use a search engine, such as www.yahooligans.com or www.internet4kids.com, and type in a keyword such as 'head lice'.

Websites

http://www.headlice.org/kids   This website has information and activities about head lice, designed by kids for kids. See a head louse in motion!

http://kidshealth.org/kid/ill_injure/sick/lice.html You can learn more about head lice and how to treat them at this website.

Glossary

abdomen   last of the three main sections of an insect

antenna   (plural: antennae) feeler on an insect's head

anus   hole in the abdomen through which droppings are passed

digest   break down food so it can be used for energy and growth

exoskeleton   hard outside skin of an insect

fertilized   insects will grow inside eggs; unfertilized eggs do not hatch

mate   when a male and a female come together to produce young

nymphs   young stage of an insect; a nymph looks similar to the adult, except smaller

proboscis   mouthpart that is a tube

saliva   liquid from the mouth

scalp   skin on part of head with the main hair growing on it

sense   how an animal knows what is going on around it

species   type or kind of animal; animals of the same species can produce young together

spine   hard, pointed spike

spiracle   tiny air hole on an insect's body, which lets air inside

thorax   chest part of an insect

Index

abdomen   8, 9, 16, 17, 20, 25

air holes   16, 20

antennae   8, 9, 14, 15

anus   21

claws   4, 19

colour   8, 17, 26

crab lice   7

dog lice   11

droppings   21

eggs   22, 23, 24, 25, 28

exoskeleton   5, 9, 27

eyes   8, 9, 14, 15

feet   18, 19

fertilization   22, 23

food   10, 11, 12, 13, 20, 21, 26

habitat   6, 7

hairs   9, 14, 15

head   8, 12, 13, 14, 15

heart   20, 21

human body lice   8

legs   4, 5, 8, 9, 18, 19

mating   22

moulting   27

mouthparts   4, 10, 11, 12, 13

nymphs   26, 27

proboscis   10, 11, 12, 13

saliva   13

senses   14, 15

sizes   4, 5, 26, 27

species   5

spines   9, 19

stomach   20, 21

teeth   10, 11, 25

thorax   8, 16, 18, 20

thumbs   19